W9-CLX-801

Earwax

by Grace Hansen

BEGINNING SCIENCE:
GROSS BODY FUNTIONS

Abdo Kids Jumbo is an Imprint of Abdo Kids
abdobooks.com

abdobooks.com

Published by Abdo Kids, a division of ABDO, P.O. Box 398166, Minneapolis, Minnesota 55439.
Copyright © 2021 by Abdo Consulting Group, Inc. International copyrights reserved in all countries.
No part of this book may be reproduced in any form without written permission from the publisher.
Abdo Kids Jumbo™ is a trademark and logo of Abdo Kids.

Printed in the United States of America, North Mankato, Minnesota.

052020

092020

Photo Credits: iStock, Science Source, Shutterstock

Production Contributors: Teddy Borth, Jennie Forsberg, Grace Hansen
Design Contributors: Dorothy Toth, Pakou Moua

Library of Congress Control Number: 2019956487
Publisher's Cataloging-in-Publication Data

Names: Hansen, Grace, author.

Title: Earwax / by Grace Hansen

Description: Minneapolis, Minnesota : Abdo Kids, 2021 | Series: Beginning science: gross body functions |
    Includes online resources and index.

Identifiers: ISBN 9781098202378 (lib. bdg.) | ISBN 9781644943847 (pbk.) | ISBN 9781098203351 (ebook)
    | ISBN 9781098203849 (Read-to-Me ebook)

Subjects: LCSH: Human body--Juvenile literature. | Earwax--Juvenile literature. | Ear--Care and hygiene—
    Juvenile literature. | Excretion--Juvenile literature. | Hygiene--Juvenile literature.

Classification: DDC 612--dc23

Table of Contents

An Earful on Earwax

Earwax can look pretty gross! But it actually has an important job to do inside the ears.

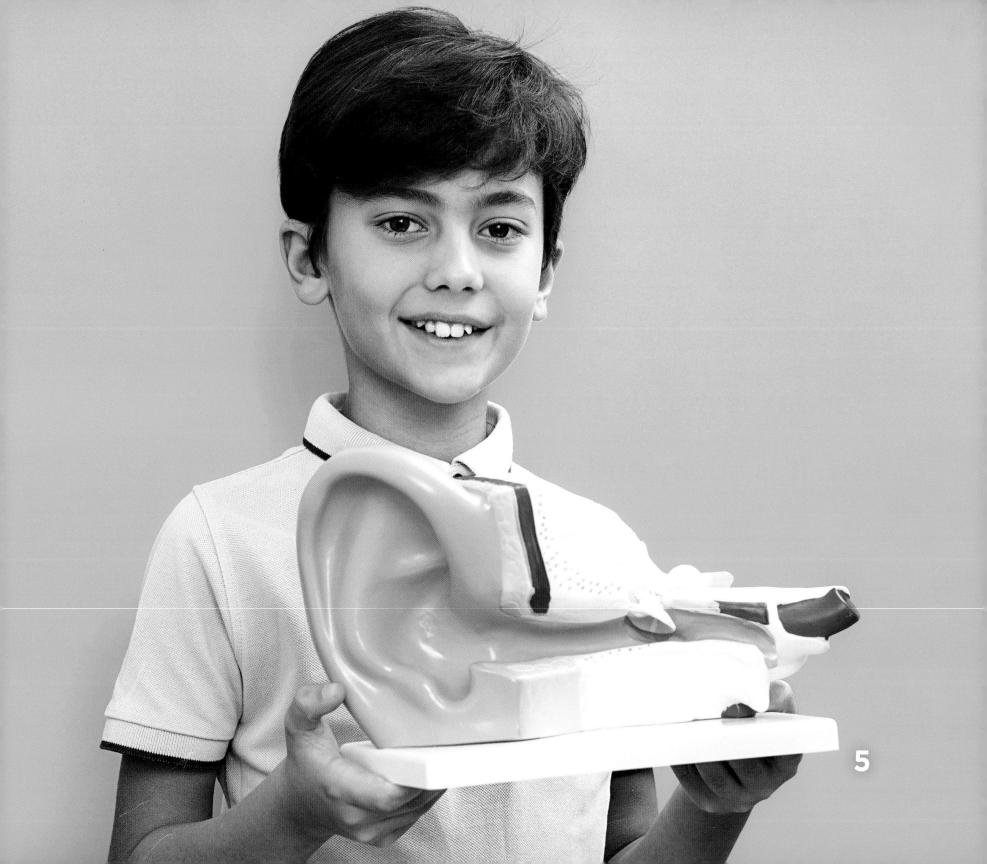

Earwax is mostly made up of fat. It is sticky and shiny.

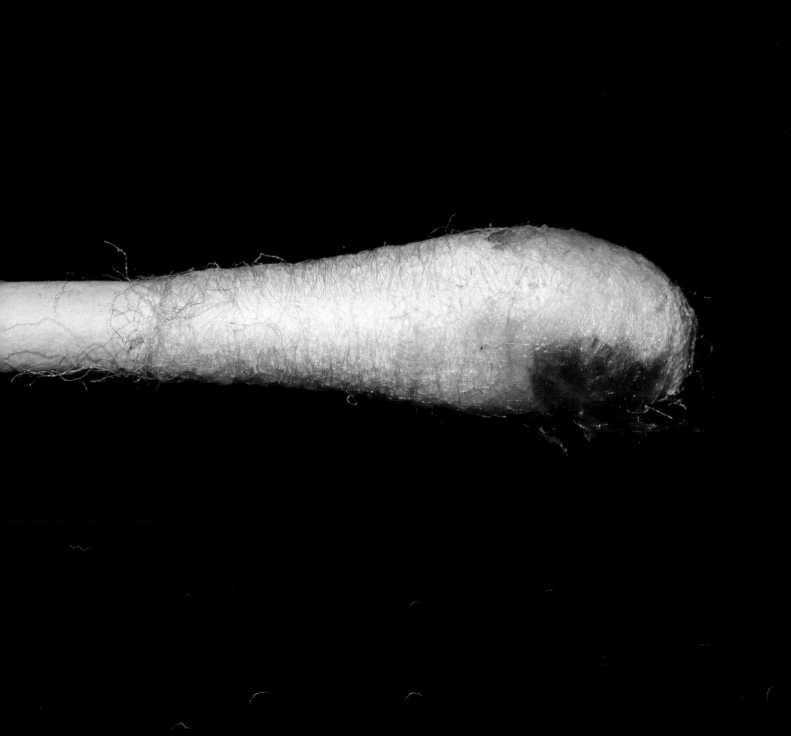

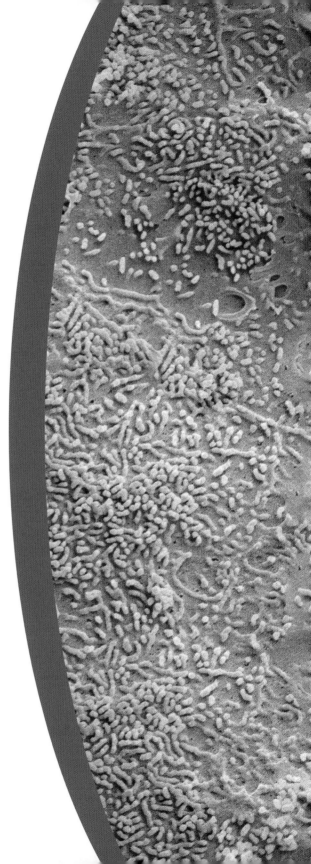

Wax **glands** make earwax. These glands are in the outer ear canal.

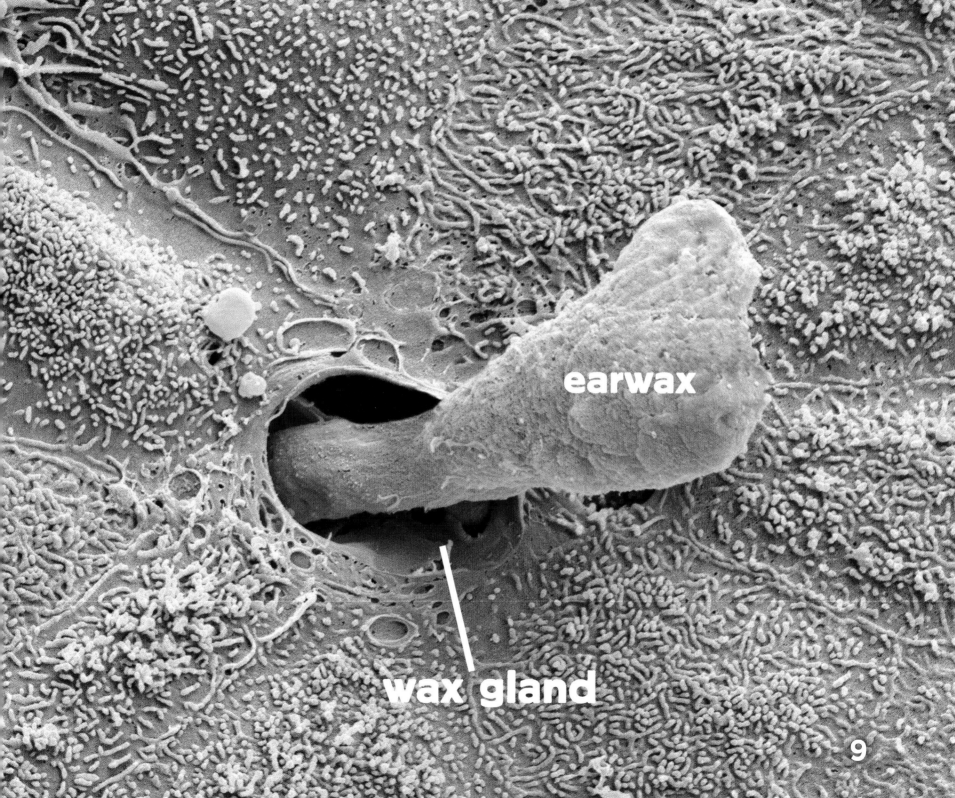

earwax

wax gland

9

Your inner ear canal is home to your eardrum. Your eardrum helps you to hear.

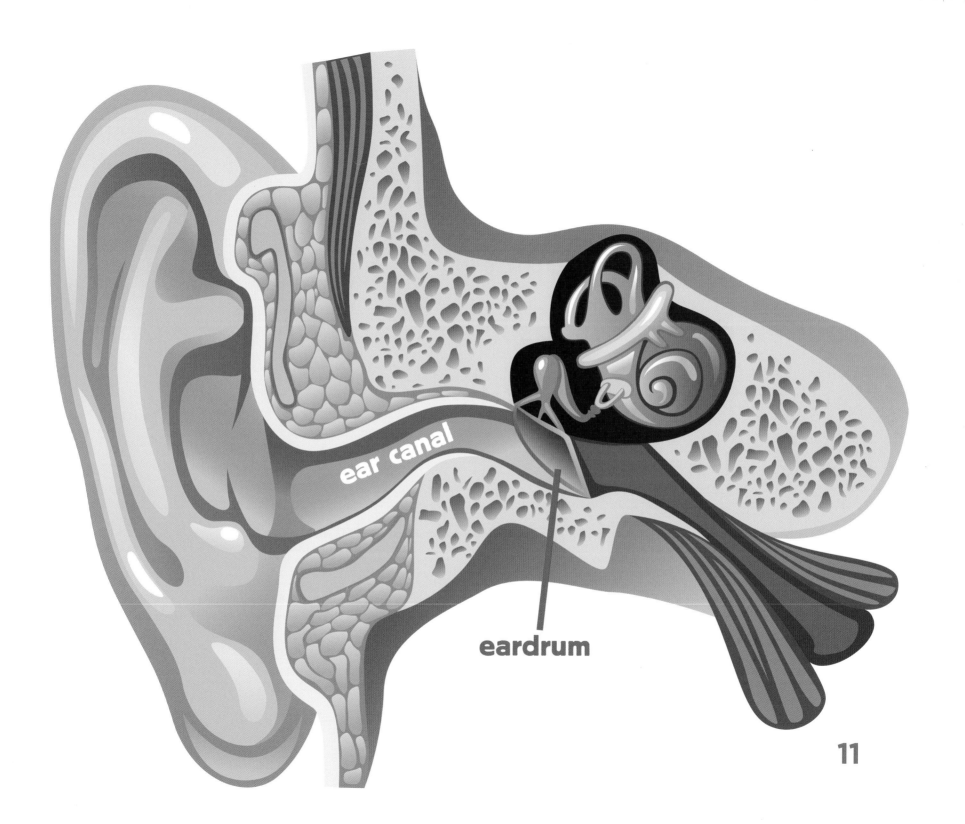

ear canal

eardrum

11

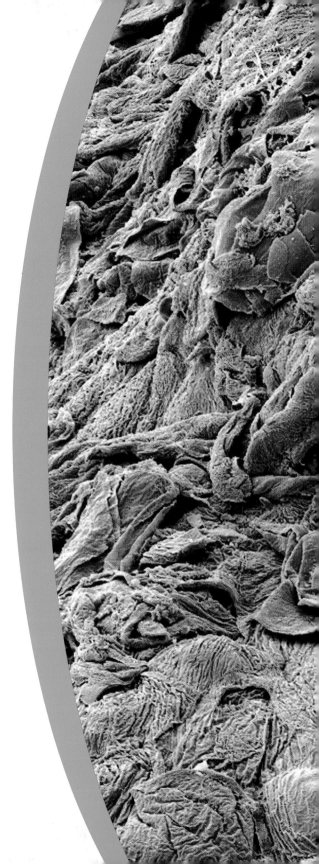

Earwax works to protect your eardrums. Things like dust and dirt can enter the ear canal. Earwax and ear hair keep these things away from the eardrum.

Earwax has special chemicals. These chemicals help fight germs. Germs can lead to ear **infections**.

earwax

Earwax also works to clean your ear canal. Earwax catches dirt and dust. Then it makes its way toward the opening of the ear.

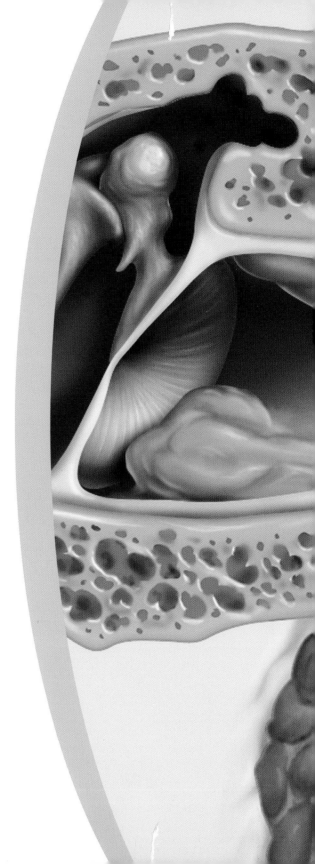

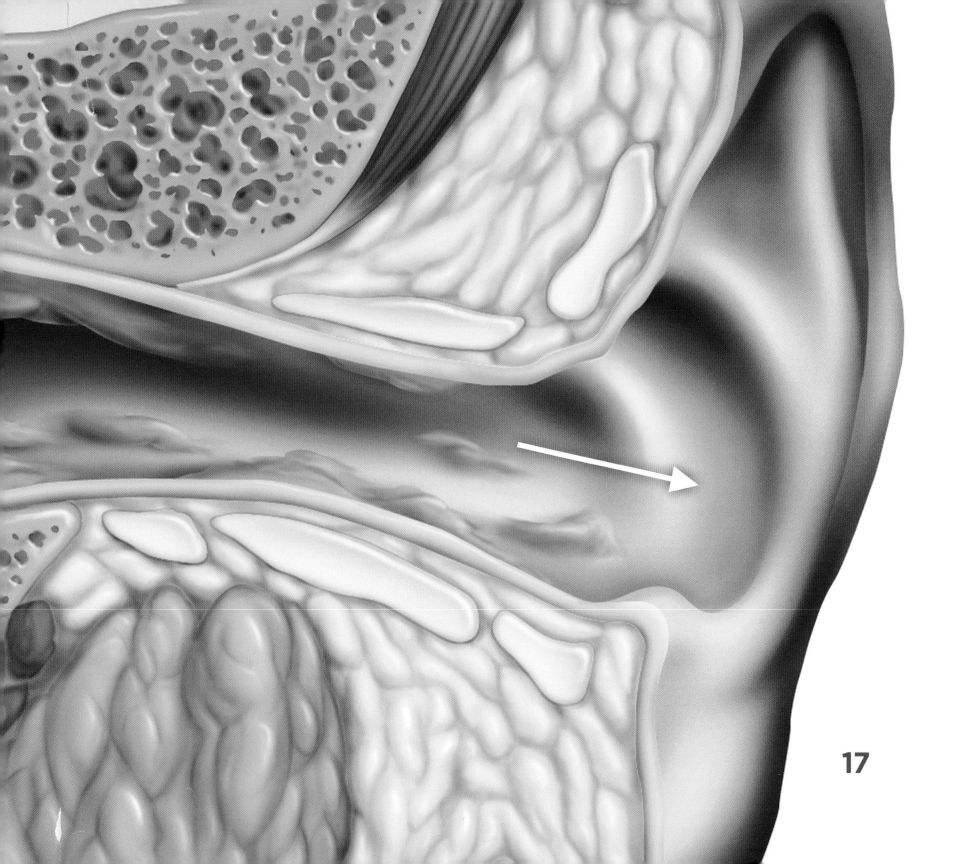

17

Earwax even helps keep your inner ears from getting too dry. Dry ears lead to itchiness.

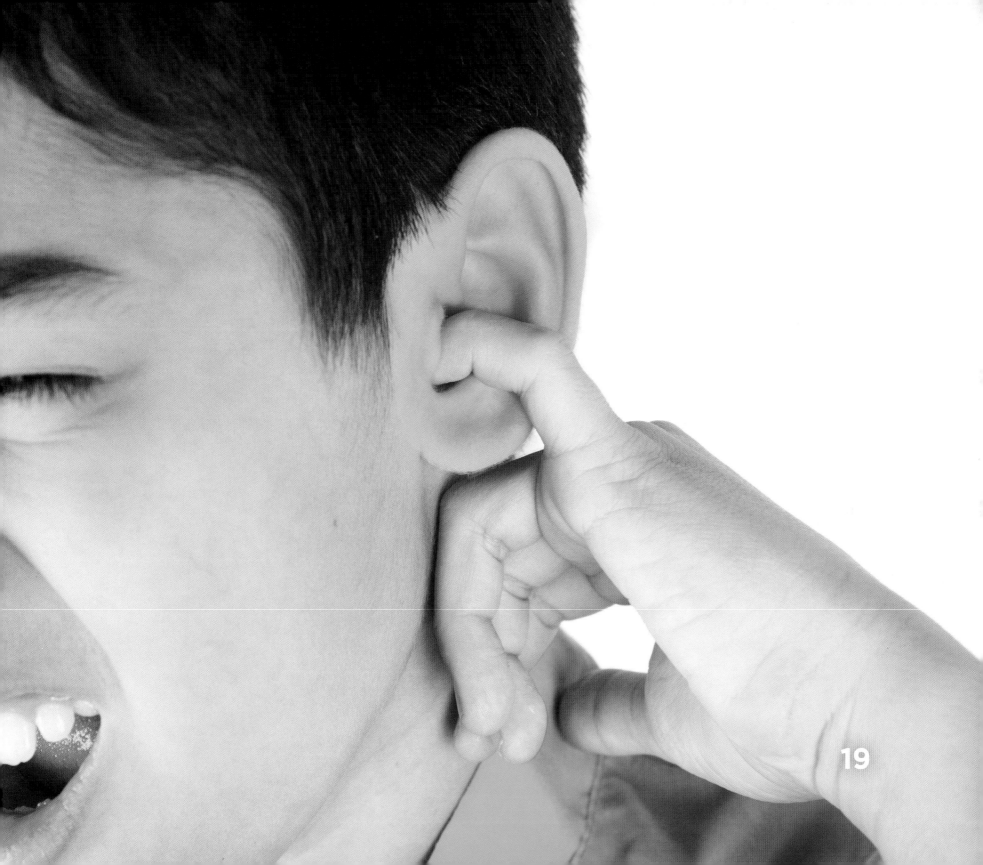

19

Ear Care

Many people think they need to remove earwax from their ear canals. But it is there to help us! Cotton swabs should only be used outside of the ear.

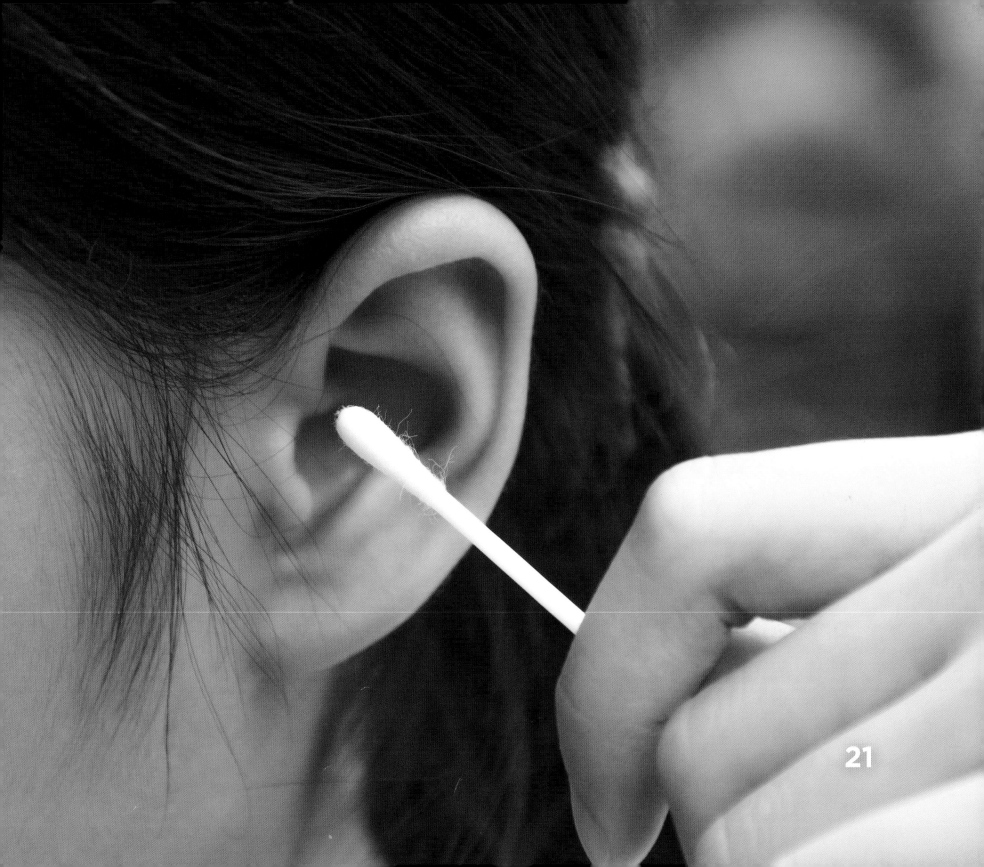

21

Let's Review!

- Earwax is made by wax **glands** in your ear canal.

- Earwax cleans, protects, and moisturizes your ears.

- Earwax has special chemicals in it that kill germs.

- Earwax is thick and sticky. It can catch things like dust and dirt.

- Earwax works to keep germs, dust, and dirt from making it to your inner ear canal.

Glossary

fat – a white or yellow oily substance found in some parts of the body.

gland – a group of cells or an organ that produces fluids that are released into the body or pass out of the body.

infection – a disease caused by germs that enter the body.

Index

Abdo Kids ONLINE
FREE! ONLINE MULTIMEDIA RESOURCES

Visit **abdokids.com**
to access crafts, games,
videos, and more!

Use Abdo Kids code

BEK2378

or scan this QR code!